A DAILY REMINDER

Love for a Lifetime

Building a Marriage
That Will Go the Distance

DR. JAMES C. DOBSON

MULTNOMAH BOOKS · SISTERS, OREGON

LOVE FOR A LIFETIME
© 1994 by Dr. James C. Dobson

Published by Multnomah Books
a part of the Questar publishing family

Printed in the United States of America

International Standard Book Number: 0- 88070-692-9

Most Scripture quotations are from the *New International Version* (©1973, 1978, 1984
by the International Bible Society; used by permission of Zondervan Publishing House).

94 95 96 97 98 99 00 01 — 10 9 8 7 6 5 4 3 2 1

Introduction

Great marriages are graced by an almost
mystical bond of friendship, unbreakable commitment,
and a deep understanding that nearly defies explanation.
A great marriage occurs when a man and a woman,
being separate and distinct individuals, are fused into a single unit
which the Bible calls "one flesh."

But getting there isn't easy, and precious few couples ever make it—
especially in this divorce-happy culture.

This little book was written to provide needed guidance.
It focuses on a few principles and concepts
that will help armor-plate a marriage and equip it to "go the distance."
Much of its sage advice was gleaned from couples who've been
married thirty, forty, even fifty years.

It highlights the major pitfalls that undermine a relationship and offers counsel on how to avoid them.

Ultimately, everything in this book relies on the principles endorsed by the Creator of families Himself.

Married life is a marathon, not a sprint.
It is not enough to make a great start toward a long-term marriage.
You will need the determination to keep plugging,
even when every fiber in your body longs to give it up.
Only then will you make it to the end.
But hang in there! Shirley and I will be waiting for you
at the finish line.

DR. JAMES DOBSON

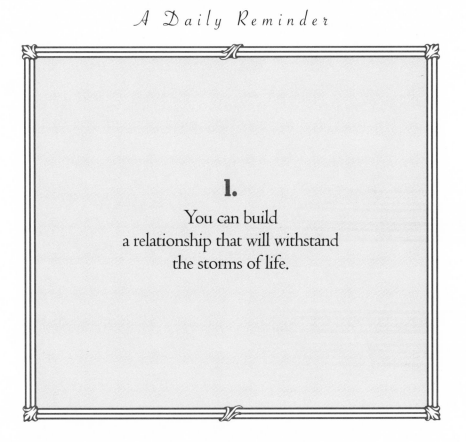

1.

You can build
a relationship that will withstand
the storms of life.

2.

Immaturity, selfishness,
hostility, vulnerability, and a sense of inadequacy
are the prime ingredients of marital instability,
and too commonly, divorce itself.
An army of disillusioned ex-husbands and
ex-wives can attest to that.

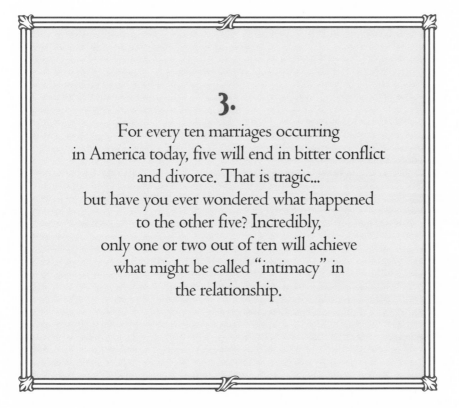

3.

For every ten marriages occurring
in America today, five will end in bitter conflict
and divorce. That is tragic...
but have you ever wondered what happened
to the other five? Incredibly,
only one or two out of ten will achieve
what might be called "intimacy" in
the relationship.

4.

Intimacy...the mystical bond of
friendship, commitment, and understanding that
almost defies explanation.
It occurs when a man and woman, being separate and
distinct individuals, are fused into a single unit which
the Bible calls "one flesh."

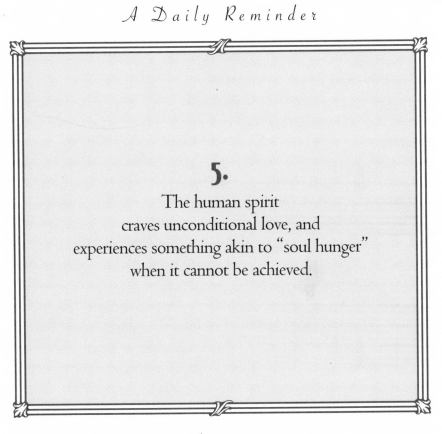

5.

The human spirit
craves unconditional love, and
experiences something akin to "soul hunger"
when it cannot be achieved.

6.

Most couples
expect to find intimacy in marriage,
but somehow it usually
eludes them.

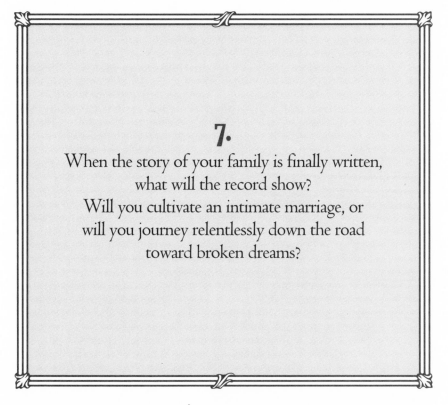

7.

When the story of your family is finally written,
what will the record show?
Will you cultivate an intimate marriage, or
will you journey relentlessly down the road
toward broken dreams?

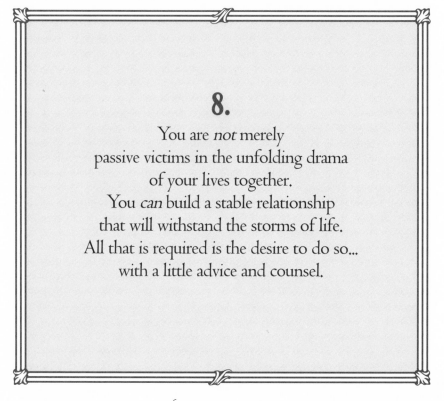

8.

You are *not* merely
passive victims in the unfolding drama
of your lives together.
You *can* build a stable relationship
that will withstand the storms of life.
All that is required is the desire to do so...
with a little advice and counsel.

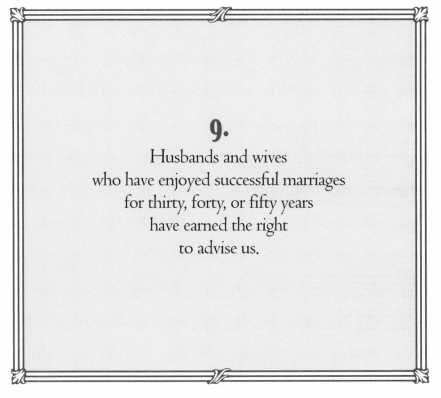

9.

Husbands and wives
who have enjoyed successful marriages
for thirty, forty, or fifty years
have earned the right
to advise us.

10.

Ultimately, of course,
we must rely on the principles endorsed
by the Creator of families Himself.
That is pretty safe counsel,
to be sure.

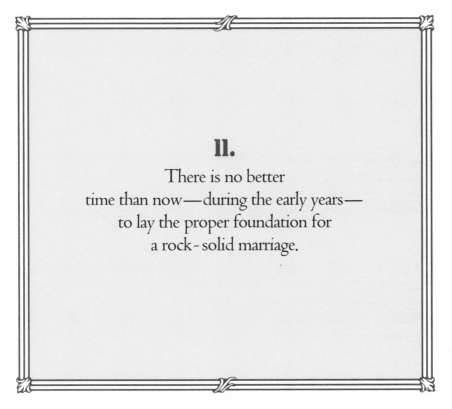

11.

There is no better
time than now—during the early years—
to lay the proper foundation for
a rock-solid marriage.

And now these three remain:
faith, hope, and love.
But the greatest of these is love.

1 CORINTHIANS 13:13

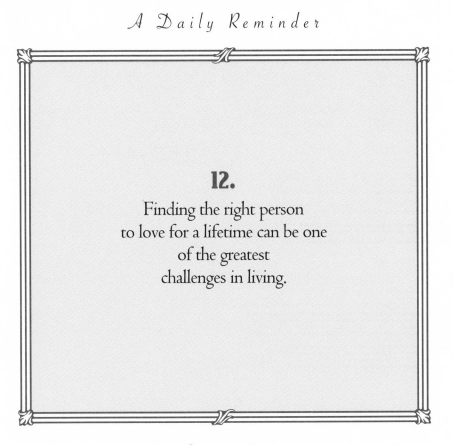

12.

Finding the right person
to love for a lifetime can be one
of the greatest
challenges in living.

13.

Many couples
come into marriage having had no
healthy role models in their formative years.
They have felt the apathy and heard the
piercing silence between their parents.
It's no wonder today's newlyweds often splutter
and fumble their way through early
married life.

14.

Popular music reflects
skepticism about long-term marriage.
The lyrics say, in effect, it is impossible to achieve
intimacy in marriage, and our life together will be
lonely, meaningless, and sterile.
How strongly I disagree with the message
in these sad songs! It's *not* true that husbands and
wives are destined to hurt and reject
one another. The family was God's idea and
He does not make mistakes.

15.

God observed the loneliness
that plagued Adam in the Garden of Eden
and said, "It is not good."
That's why He gave him a woman to share
his thoughts and feel
his touch.

16.

Marriage is a marvelous concept
when functioning as intended, but therein
lies the problem.
We have fallen into certain behavioral
patterns that weaken the marriage and interfere
with long-term relationships.

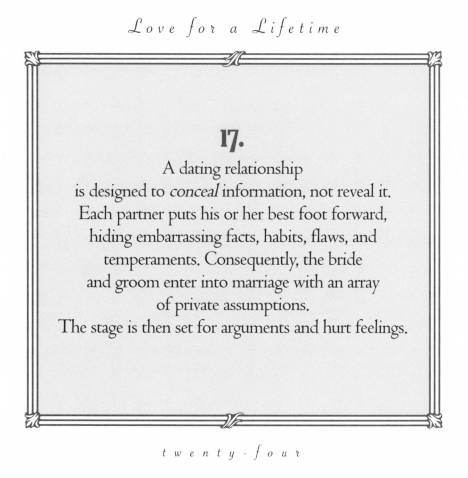

17.

A dating relationship
is designed to *conceal* information, not reveal it.
Each partner puts his or her best foot forward,
hiding embarrassing facts, habits, flaws, and
temperaments. Consequently, the bride
and groom enter into marriage with an array
of private assumptions.
The stage is then set for arguments and hurt feelings.

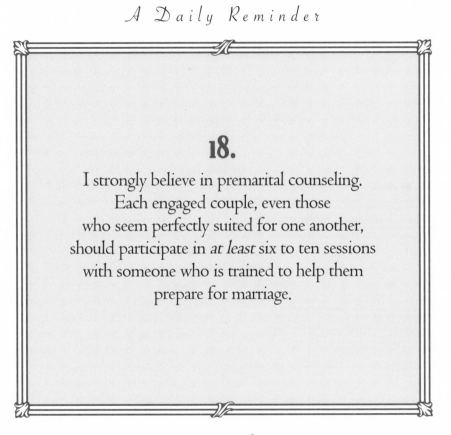

18.

I strongly believe in premarital counseling.
Each engaged couple, even those
who seem perfectly suited for one another,
should participate in *at least* six to ten sessions
with someone who is trained to help them
prepare for marriage.

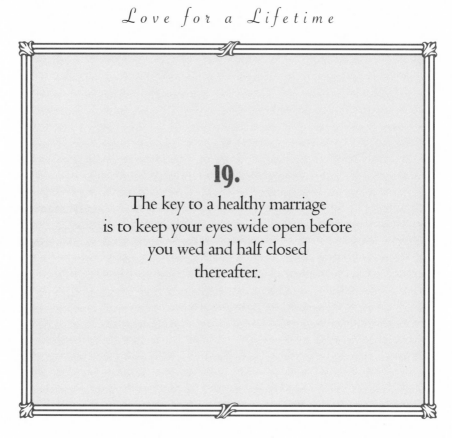

19.

The key to a healthy marriage
is to keep your eyes wide open before
you wed and half closed
thereafter.

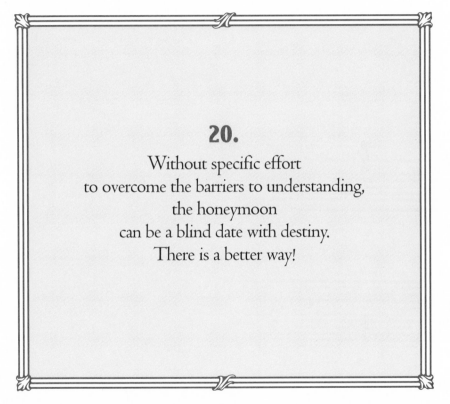

20.

Without specific effort
to overcome the barriers to understanding,
the honeymoon
can be a blind date with destiny.
There is a better way!

Knowledge puffs up,
but love builds up.

1 CORINTHIANS 8:16

21.

Even those outside the Christian faith
now agree that the sexual revolution was
an unmitigated disaster.
As it turns out, abstinence before marriage,
and life-long fidelity were
pretty good ideas after all.

22.

Some sociologists
are rediscovering the benefits
of sexual restraint—as though
they had stumbled onto a
brand new concept.

23.

There is no such thing as "safe sex"
just as there is no safe sin!
When a person chooses to live in direct contradiction
to the laws of God,
there is no place to hide.

24.

Virginity before marriage is the best foundation.
That's the way the system was designed by the Creator
and no one has yet devised a way to improve
on His plan.

25.

How could we have *expected* to preserve
the symbiotic relationships between men and women
when the rules governing our sexual behavior
were turned upside down?
Family disintegration was inevitable.

26.

Bonding refers to the emotional covenant
that links a man and woman together for life
and makes them intensely valuable to each other.
It is the specialness that sets those two lovers apart
from every other couple on the face of the earth.
It is God's gift of companionship to those
who have experienced it.

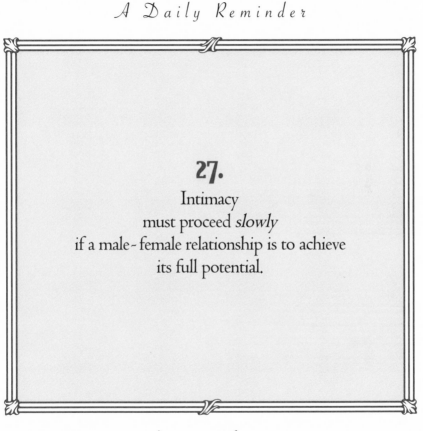

27.
Intimacy
must proceed *slowly*
if a male-female relationship is to achieve
its full potential.

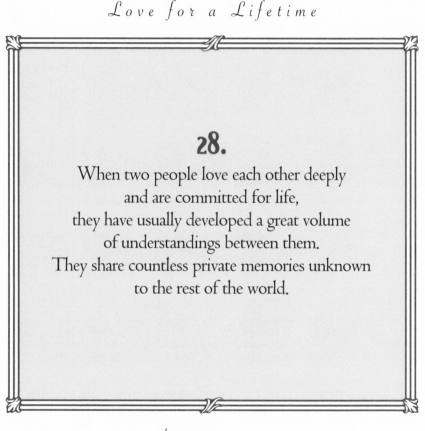

28.

When two people love each other deeply
and are committed for life,
they have usually developed a great volume
of understandings between them.
They share countless private memories unknown
to the rest of the world.

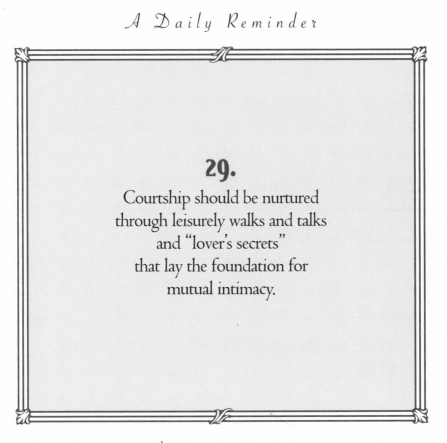

29.

Courtship should be nurtured
through leisurely walks and talks
and "lover's secrets"
that lay the foundation for
mutual intimacy.

*Let us not love with words or tongue
but with actions and in truth.*

1 JOHN 3:18

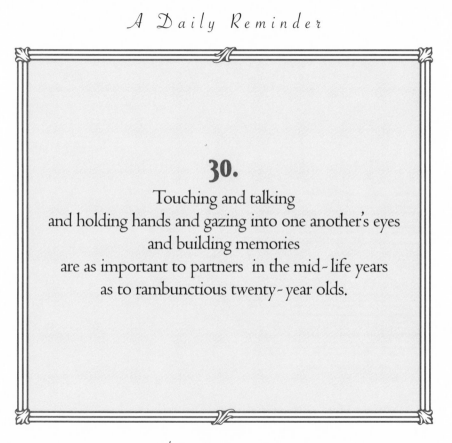

30.
Touching and talking
and holding hands and gazing into one another's eyes
and building memories
are as important to partners in the mid- life years
as to rambunctious twenty- year olds.

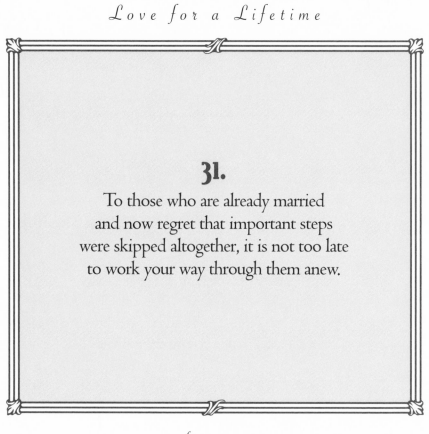

31.

To those who are already married
and now regret that important steps
were skipped altogether, it is not too late
to work your way through them anew.

32.

Don't rush the courtship period
when you feel you have found the "one and only."
Frank Sinatra said it musically,
"Take it nice and easy,
making all the stops along the way."

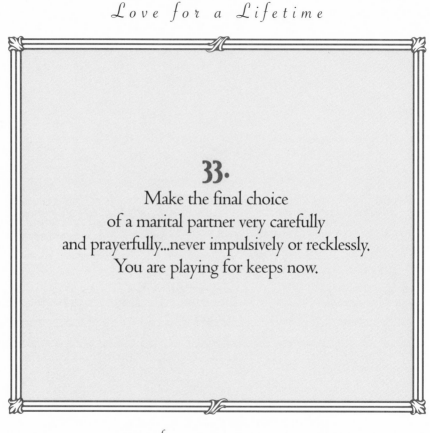

33.

Make the final choice
of a marital partner very carefully
and prayerfully...never impulsively or recklessly.
You are playing for keeps now.

34.

Bring to bear every ounce
of intelligence and discretion available to you
as you select your marriage partner,
and then yield the ultimate decision to
the will of the Lord. He will guide you if you
don't run ahead of Him.

35.

Enter the marriage bed as a virgin.
If it's too late to preserve your virginity,
initiate a policy of abstinence today,
and don't waver from it
until you are wed.

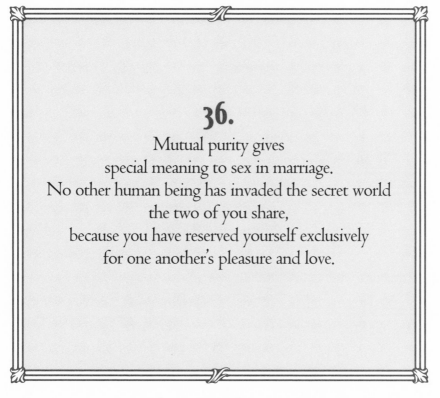

36.
Mutual purity gives
special meaning to sex in marriage.
No other human being has invaded the secret world
the two of you share,
because you have reserved yourself exclusively
for one another's pleasure and love.

37.

It is known now
that when you sleep with a promiscuous partner,
you are having sex with every person
that individual has slept with
in the past ten years!
Virginity before marriage is by far the
healthiest approach.

38.
Remain faithful
to your partner for life.
No exceptions!

Bear with each other and forgive
whatever grievances you may have
against one another.
Forgive as the Lord forgave you.
And over all these virtues put on love,
which binds them all together
in perfect unity.

COLOSSIANS 3:13, 14

39.

It is important to understand
the ways men and women are unique
if we hope to
live together in harmony.
Genesis tells us that the Creator made *two* sexes,
not one, and that He designed each gender
for a specific purpose.

40.

Eve, being suited to Adam's particular needs,
was given to him as a "help-meet."
How unfortunate has been
the recent effort to deny this uniqueness and
homogenate the human family!
It simply won't square with the facts.

41.

The sexes are blessed
with a vast array of unique emotional characteristics.
It is a wise and dedicated husband
who desires to understand
his wife's psychological needs and then sets out to
meet them.

42.
Young husbands
must comprehend how their wives are unique,
and how their particular needs are related to
happiness or depression
in marriage.

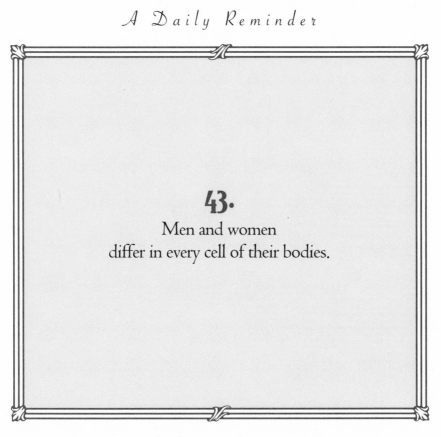

43.

Men and women
differ in every cell of their bodies.

44.

Briefly stated,
love is linked to self-esteem
in women.

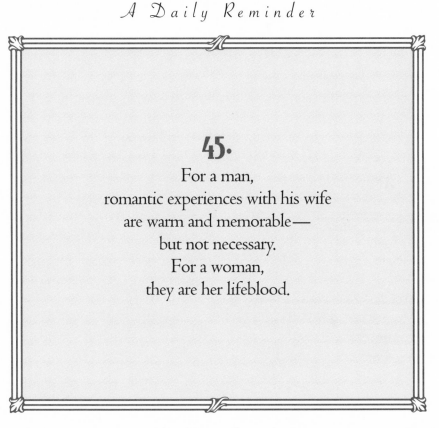

45.
For a man,
romantic experiences with his wife
are warm and memorable—
but not necessary.
For a woman,
they are her lifeblood.

However, each one of you also must
love his wife as he loves himself,
and the wife must respect her husband.

EPHESIANS 5:33

46.

A woman's confidence,
her sexual response, and her zest for living
are often directly related
to those tender moments when she feels deeply loved
and appreciated by her man.
That is why flowers and candy and cards are more
meaningful to her than to him.

47.

This need for romantic love
is not some quirk or peculiarity of a wife,
as some men may think.
This is the way women are made.

48.

Men need to understand
that women tend to care more than they
about the home and everything in it.
Husbands sometimes fail to comprehend
the *significance* of this inclination.

49.
One masculine need
comes to mind which wives should not fail to heed.
It reflects what men want most
in their homes:
tranquillity.

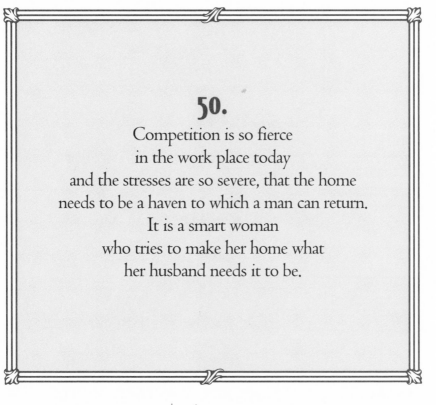

50.
Competition is so fierce
in the work place today
and the stresses are so severe, that the home
needs to be a haven to which a man can return.
It is a smart woman
who tries to make her home what
her husband needs it to be.

51.

I'm convinced that emotional instability
and even physical illness can occur in the absence
of a tranquil "safe place" within the home.
Creating an environment to meet that need
should be given priority,
regardless of the family structure.

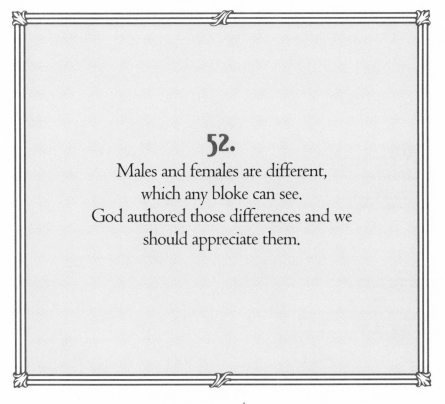

52.
Males and females are different,
which any bloke can see.
God authored those differences and we
should appreciate them.

53.

It is our uniqueness
that gives freshness and vitality to a relationship.
How boring it would be if the sexes
were identical, as the radical feminists
have tried to tell us!

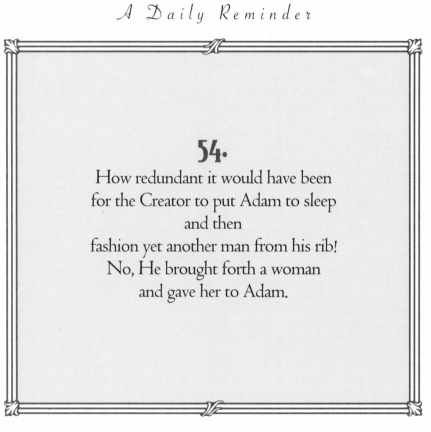

54.

How redundant it would have been
for the Creator to put Adam to sleep
and then
fashion yet another man from his rib!
No, He brought forth a woman
and gave her to Adam.

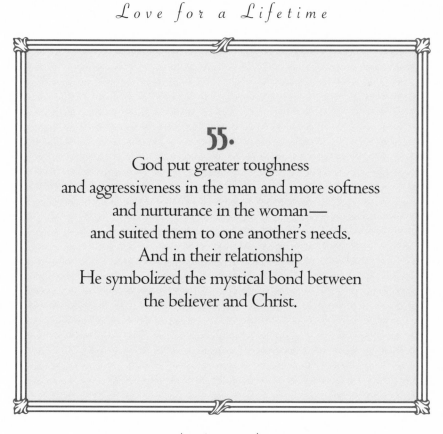

55.

God put greater toughness
and aggressiveness in the man and more softness
and nurturance in the woman—
and suited them to one another's needs.
And in their relationship
He symbolized the mystical bond between
the believer and Christ.

56.
Husbands and wives,
celebrate your uniquenesses and learn to
compromise when male and female
individuality collide.

...then make my joy complete
by being like-minded,
having the same love,
being one in spirit and in purpose.

PHILLIPIANS 2:2

57.

An unnamed Frenchman
once said, "Vive la difference!"
He must have been
a happily married man.

58.

Newlyweds should establish
and maintain
a *Christ-centered home.*
Everything rests on that foundation.

59.

A young husband and wife
deeply committed to Jesus Christ
enjoy enormous advantages
over the family with
no spiritual dimension.

60.

A meaningful prayer life
is essential
in maintaining
a Christ-centered home.

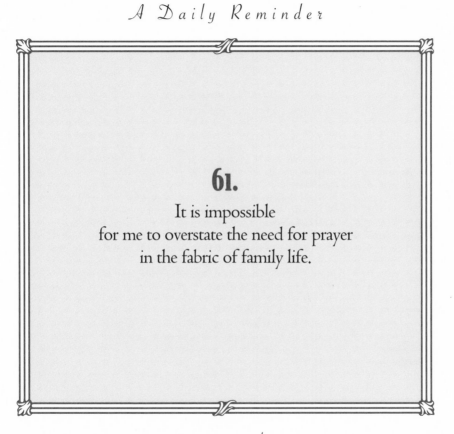

61.

It is impossible
for me to overstate the need for prayer
in the fabric of family life.

62.

A personal relationship
with Jesus Christ is the cornerstone of marriage,
giving meaning and purpose to every
dimension of living.

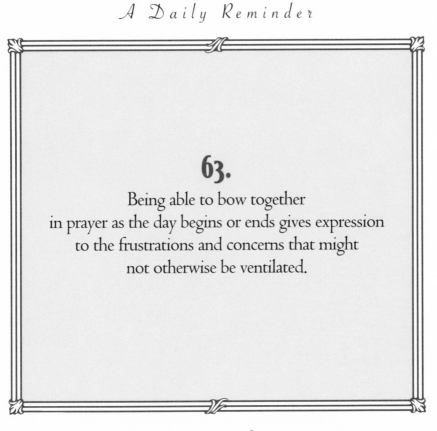

63.

Being able to bow together
in prayer as the day begins or ends gives expression
to the frustrations and concerns that might
not otherwise be ventilated.

64.

In this day of disintegrating families
on every side, we dare not try to make it
on our own.

65.

The couple who depends on Scripture
for solutions to the stresses of living
has a distinct advantage
over the family with no faith.
By reading these holy words, we are given a
"window" into the mind of the Father.
What an incredible resource!

But I will sing of your strength,
in the morning I will sing of your love;
for you are my fortress,
my refuge in times of trouble.

PSALM 59:16

66.

The Creator who began with nothingness
and made beautiful mountains and streams and clouds
and cuddly little babies has elected to give us
the inside story of the family.
Marriage and parenting were His ideas,
and He tells in His Word how to live together
in peace and harmony.

67.

Everything from handling money
to sexual attitudes is discussed in Scripture,
with each prescription
bearing the personal endorsement
of the King of the Universe.
Why would anyone disregard this
ultimate resource?

68.

The Christian way of life
lends stability to marriage because
its principles
and values naturally produce
harmony.

69.

When put into action,
Christian teaching emphasizes giving to others,
self-discipline, obedience to divine commandments,
conformity to the laws of man,
and love and fidelity between a
husband and wife.

70.

You probably knelt together
and shared a prayer
during your wedding ceremony.
Return to the source daily for
strength and stability.

My command is this:
Love each other as I have loved you.

JOHN 15:12

71.

Marriages
that lack an iron-willed determination to hang
together at all costs
are like fragile Roman bridges.
They *appear* to be secure
and may indeed remain upright...until
they are put under heavy pressure.
That's when the seams split and the
foundation crumbles.

72.
Minor irritants,
when accumulated over time,
may even be more threatening to a marriage
than the catastrophic events that
crash into our lives.

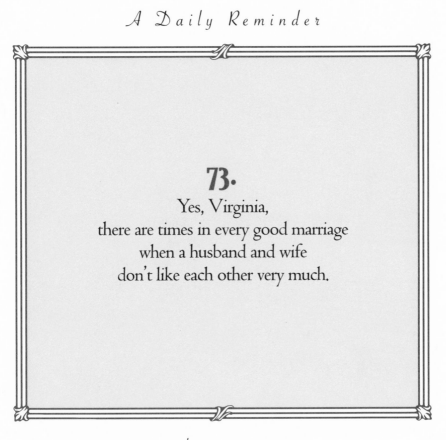

73.
Yes, Virginia,
there are times in every good marriage
when a husband and wife
don't like each other very much.

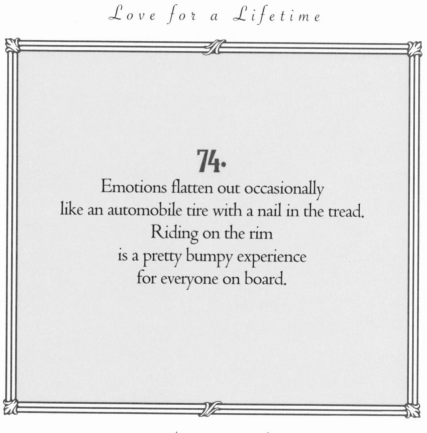

74.

Emotions flatten out occasionally
like an automobile tire with a nail in the tread.
Riding on the rim
is a pretty bumpy experience
for everyone on board.

75.
Newlyweds:
Don't count on having a placid relationship.
There *will* be times of conflict and disagreement.
There *will* be periods of emotional blandness
when you can generate nothing but a yawn
for one another.
That's life, as they say.

76.

What will you do when
unexpected tornadoes blow through your home,
or when the doldrums
leave your sails sagging and silent?
Will you pack it in and go home to Mama?
Will you pout and cry and seek ways to strike back?
Or will your commitment
hold steady?

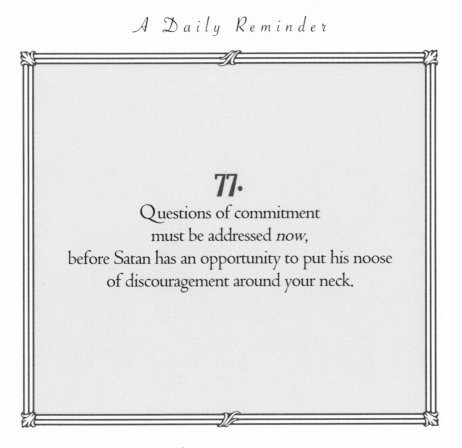

77.

Questions of commitment
must be addressed *now*,
before Satan has an opportunity to put his noose
of discouragement around your neck.

78.

Set your jaw and clench your fists.
Nothing short of death must ever be permitted
to come between the two of you.
Nothing!

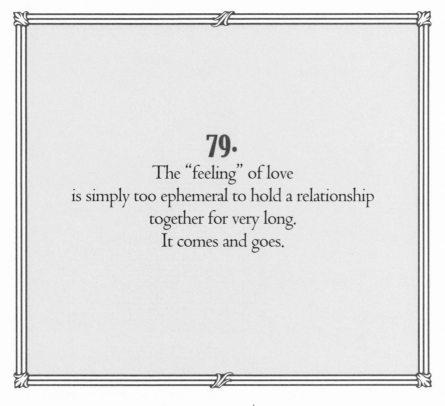

79.

The "feeling" of love
is simply too ephemeral to hold a relationship
together for very long.
It comes and goes.

*Love does not delight in evil
but rejoices in truth,
It always protects, always trusts,
always hopes, always perseveres.*

1 CORINTHIANS 13:6-7

80.

Two people are not compatible
simply because they love each other and are
both professing Christians.
Many young couples assume that the sunshine
and flowers that characterized their
courtship will continue for the rest of their lives.
Don't you believe it!

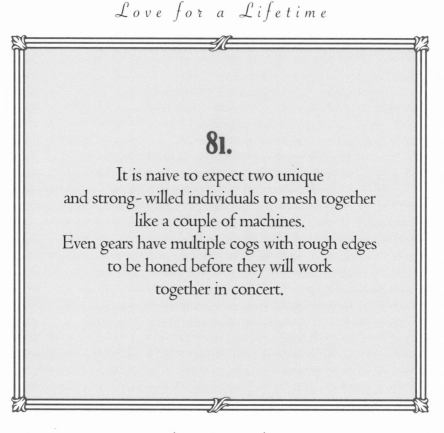

81.

It is naive to expect two unique
and strong-willed individuals to mesh together
like a couple of machines.
Even gears have multiple cogs with rough edges
to be honed before they will work
together in concert.

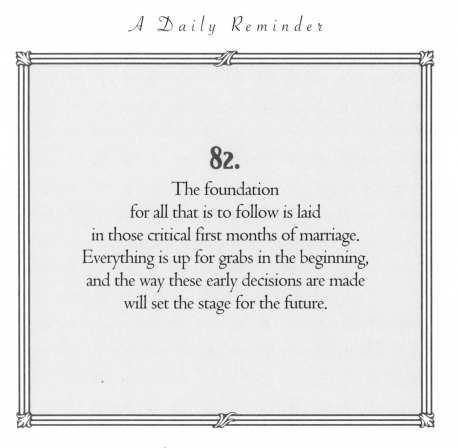

82.

The foundation
for all that is to follow is laid
in those critical first months of marriage.
Everything is up for grabs in the beginning,
and the way these early decisions are made
will set the stage for the future.

83.

One verse contains more wisdom
than most marriage manuals combined:
"Do nothing out of selfish ambition or vain conceit,
but in humility consider others
better than yourselves."

PHILIPPIANS 2:3

84.

Research
makes it clear that little girls are blessed
with greater linguistic ability than little boys,
and it remains a lifelong talent.
As an adult, she expresses her feelings and thoughts
far better than her husband and is often irritated
by his reticence.

85.

Every knowledgeable marriage counselor
knows that the inability or unwillingness
of husbands
to reveal their feelings to their wives
is one of the common complaints of women.

86.

It can almost be stated as an absolute:
Show me a quiet, reserved husband
and I'll show you a
frustrated wife.

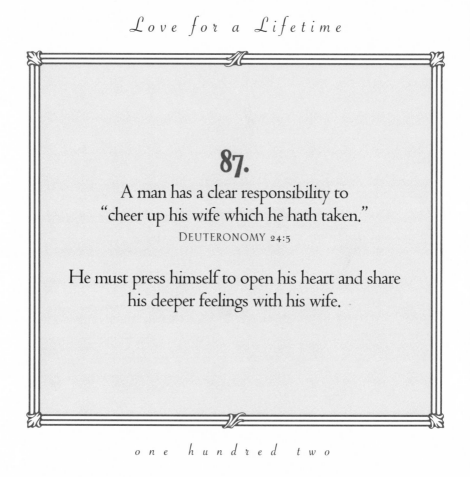

87.

A man has a clear responsibility to
"cheer up his wife which he hath taken."

DEUTERONOMY 24:5

He must press himself to open his heart and share
his deeper feelings with his wife.

88.

Time *must* be reserved in marriage
for meaningful conversations.
Taking walks and going out to breakfast
and riding bicycles on Saturday mornings
are conversation inducers
that keep love alive.

89.

Communication *can* occur
even in families where the husband leans inward
and the wife leans outward. In these instances,
I believe, the primary responsibility
for compromise lies with
the husband.

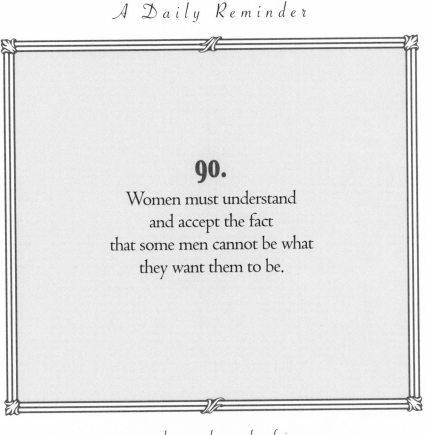

90.

Women must understand
and accept the fact
that some men cannot be what
they want them to be.

91.

Create the best marriage possible
from the raw materials brought by two imperfect
human beings with two distinctly
unique personalities.
But for all the rough edges that can never
be smoothed, try to develop the best possible
perspective and determine in your mind
to accept reality exactly as it is.

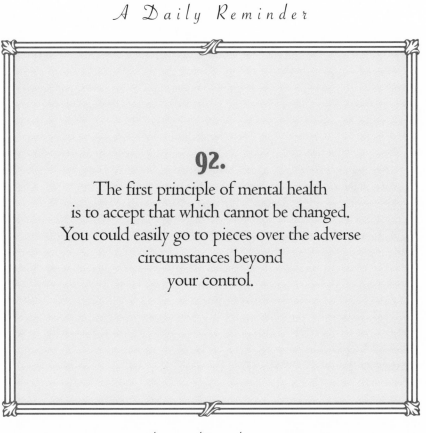

92.
The first principle of mental health
is to accept that which cannot be changed.
You could easily go to pieces over the adverse
circumstances beyond
your control.

But the fruit of the Spirit is love,
joy, peace, patience, kindness, goodness,
faithfulness, gentleness and self-control.

GALATIANS 5:22

93.

Can you accept the fact
that your husband will never be able to meet
all of your needs and aspirations?
Seldom does one human being satisfy every longing
and hope in the breast of another.

94.

Your husband is no more
equipped to resolve your entire package of
emotional needs than you are to become his sexual
dream machine every twenty-four hours.
Both partners have to settle for
human foibles and faults and irritability
and occasional nighttime
"headaches."

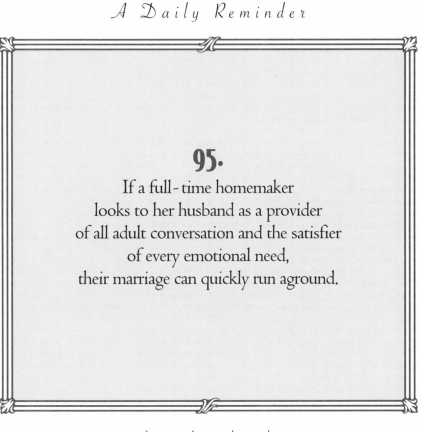

95.

If a full-time homemaker
looks to her husband as a provider
of all adult conversation and the satisfier
of every emotional need,
their marriage can quickly run aground.

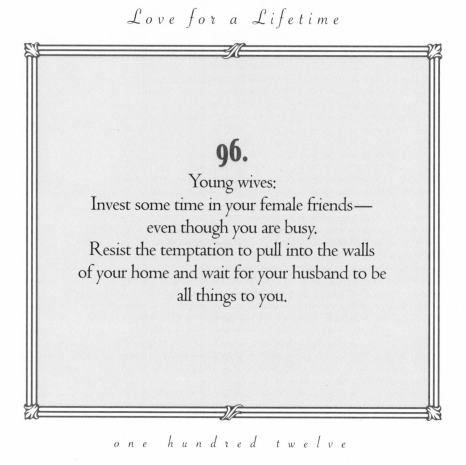

96.
Young wives:
Invest some time in your female friends—
even though you are busy.
Resist the temptation to pull into the walls
of your home and wait for your husband to be
all things to you.

97.
We are designed
to love God and to love one another.
Deprivation of either
function can be devastating.

98.

Materialism and debt
have devastated more families
than perhaps
any other factor.

99.
Men and women
tend to have different value systems
which precipitate arguments
about money.

100.

Couples need to label their credit cards:

"Danger—
Handle with Care!"

101.

A budget
is nothing more than a plan.
It doesn't limit expenditures,
it defines them.

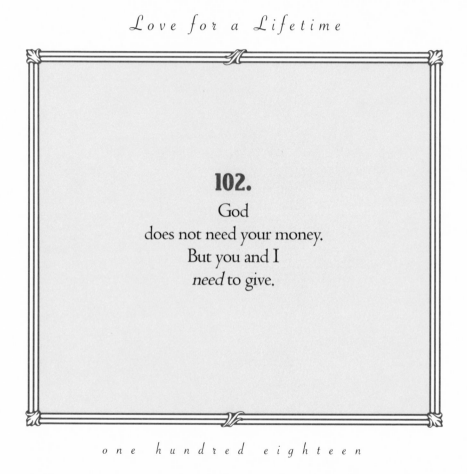

102.
God
does not need your money.
But you and I
need to give.

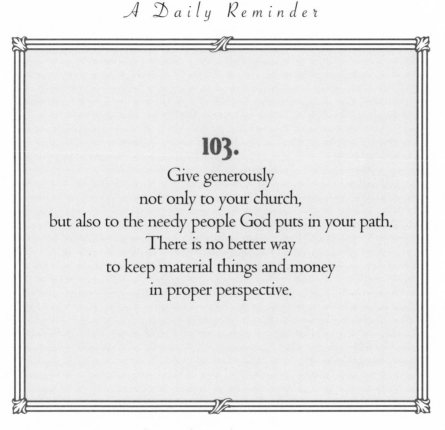

103.

Give generously
not only to your church,
but also to the needy people God puts in your path.
There is no better way
to keep material things and money
in proper perspective.

104.

Don't be surprised if sexual intercourse
is less intense than anticipated on the honeymoon.
For those who have saved themselves
for that first night, their level of expectation
may exceed reality by a
wide margin.

105.

When it comes to sex,
the transformation from
"Thou shalt not" to "Thou shalt,
regularly and with great passion" is not so easily
made by some people.
It takes time for one mindset to give way
to another.

106.

Sexual intercourse
in human beings is a highly complex mental process.
Frame of mind, setting, sense of security,
aromas, visualizations, the partner's attitude,
and one's own modesty all
come into play.

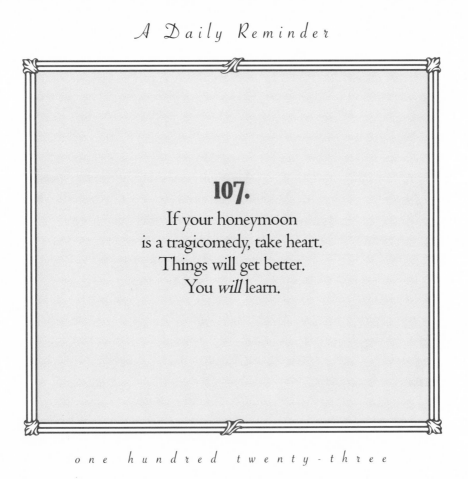

107.
If your honeymoon
is a tragicomedy, take heart.
Things will get better.
You *will* learn.

108.

Sex can still be exciting
and new after thirty or forty years of marriage
because individuals are continuing to learn
how to please themselves and
one another.

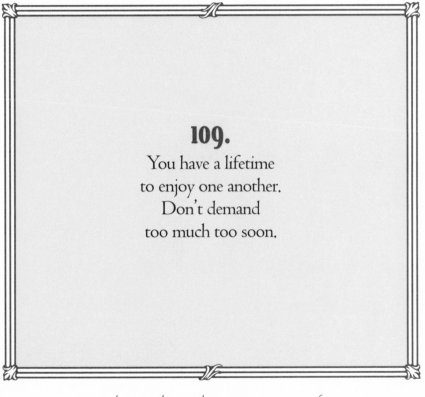

109.
You have a lifetime
to enjoy one another.
Don't demand
too much too soon.

[Love] burns like a blazing fire;
like a mighty flame.
Many waters cannot quench love;
rivers cannot wash it away.

SONG OF SONGS 8:7

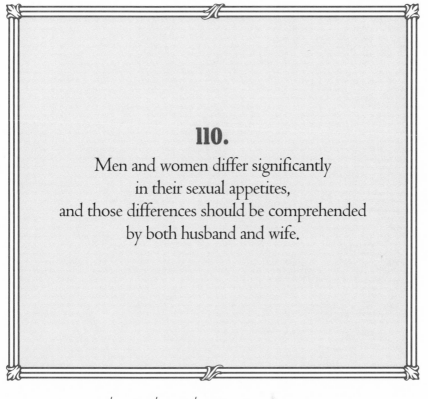

110.

Men and women differ significantly
in their sexual appetites,
and those differences should be comprehended
by both husband and wife.

111.

The way a woman feels
about her husband sexually
is a by-product
of their romantic relationship at the time.

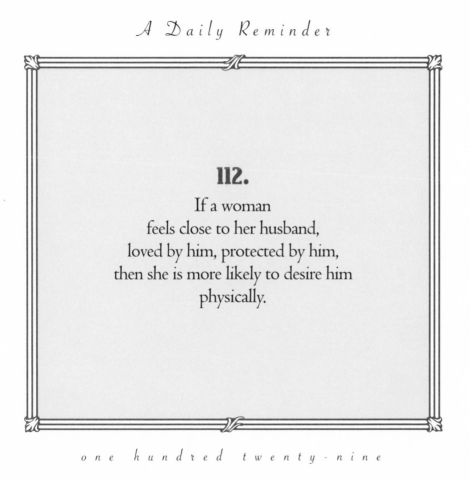

112.

If a woman
feels close to her husband,
loved by him, protected by him,
then she is more likely to desire him
physically.

113.

The surge of passion
derives from his touch
and tenderness
toward her.

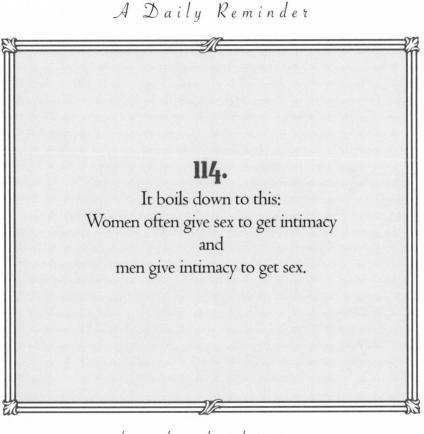

114.

It boils down to this:
Women often give sex to get intimacy
and
men give intimacy to get sex.

115.

Because women are more
romantically inclined, the man who wants
an exciting sexual relationship with his wife should
focus on the *other* 23 1/2 hours
in the day.

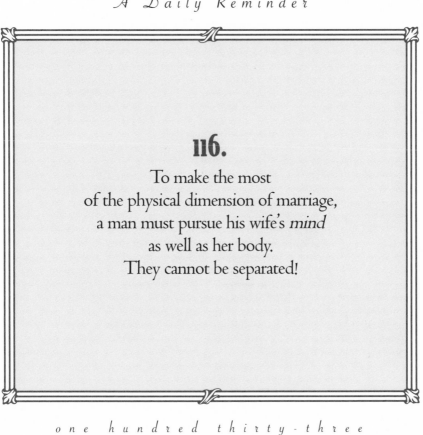

116.

To make the most
of the physical dimension of marriage,
a man must pursue his wife's *mind*
as well as her body.
They cannot be separated!

Love is patient, love is kind.
It does not envy, it does not boast,
it is not proud.
It is not rude, it is not self-seeking,
it is not easily angered,
it keeps no record of wrongs.

1 CORINTHIANS 13:4, 5

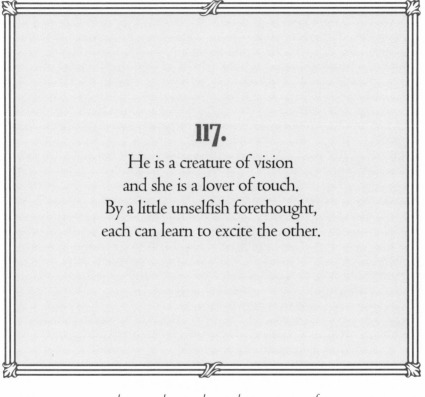

117.

He is a creature of vision
and she is a lover of touch.
By a little unselfish forethought,
each can learn to excite the other.

118.

Sex is at its best
when both partners are "lost"
in the excitement
of
unselfconscious passion.

119.

There is no real satisfaction
in mating with a stranger.
An alley cat can do that.
The real challenge
is in achieving
a monogamous, loving, caring, romantic,
mutually satisfying union.

120.

Divorce brings such loneliness
to children that its pain is difficult to describe
or even contemplate...
time does not heal their wounds.

121.

I would not minimize
the distressing "soul hunger" that women
so frequently describe,
but I will say this: Divorce is not
the answer to it!

122.

Don't permit the possibility
of divorce to enter your thinking.
Even in moments of great conflict and
discouragement, divorce is
no solution.

123.
Divorce
merely substitutes a new set of miseries
for the ones left behind.

124.

Guard your relationship
against erosion
as though you were defending
your very lives.

125.

Yes, you can make it together.
Not only can you survive, but you can keep
your love alive if you give it priority in your
system of values.

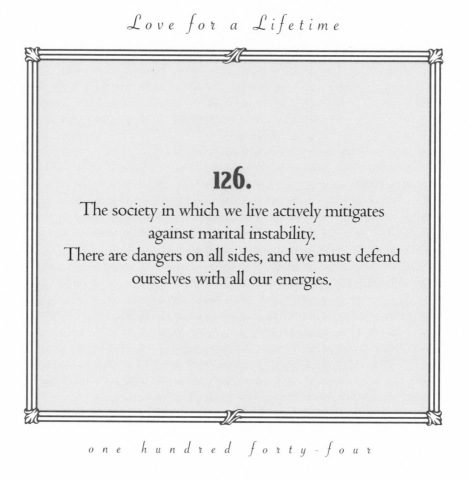

126.

The society in which we live actively mitigates
against marital instability.
There are dangers on all sides, and we must defend
ourselves with all our energies.

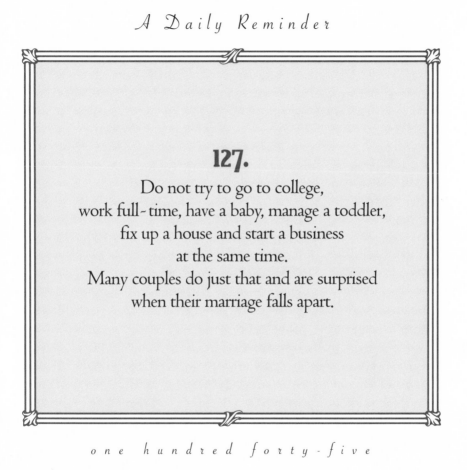

127.

Do not try to go to college,
work full-time, have a baby, manage a toddler,
fix up a house and start a business
at the same time.
Many couples do just that and are surprised
when their marriage falls apart.

128.

Pay cash
for consumable items
or don't buy.
Allocate your funds with the
wisdom of Solomon.

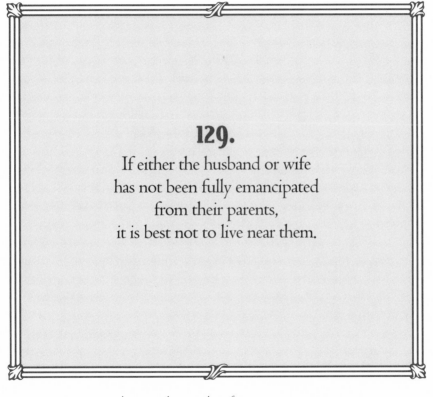

129.

If either the husband or wife
has not been fully emancipated
from their parents,
it is best not to live near them.

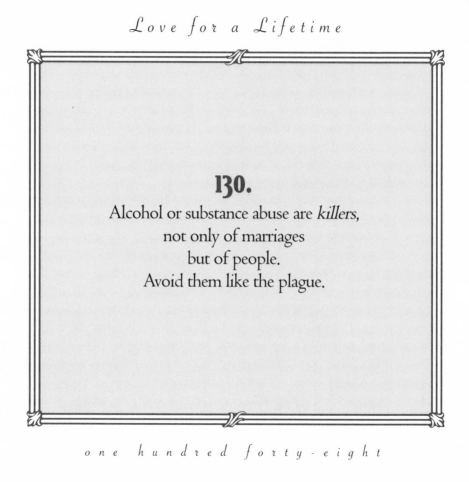

130.

Alcohol or substance abuse are *killers*,
not only of marriages
but of people.
Avoid them like the plague.

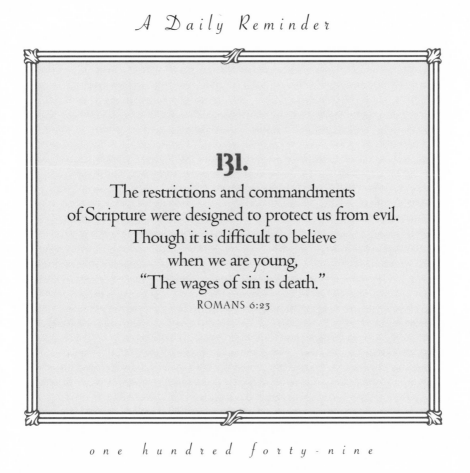

131.

The restrictions and commandments
of Scripture were designed to protect us from evil.
Though it is difficult to believe
when we are young,
"The wages of sin is death."

ROMANS 6:23

132.

The pressures of adolescence
and the stress of early married life
do not mix well.
Finish the first before taking on
the second.

133.

All that is needed to grow
the most vigorous weeds is a small crack in
your sidewalk. If you are going to beat
the odds and maintain an intimate,
long-term marriage,
you must take the weeding task
seriously.

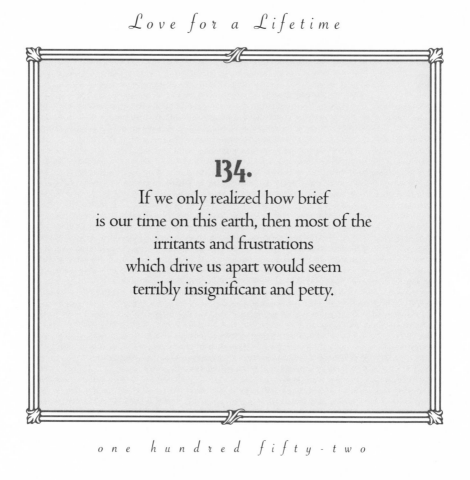

134.

If we only realized how brief
is our time on this earth, then most of the
irritants and frustrations
which drive us apart would seem
terribly insignificant and petty.

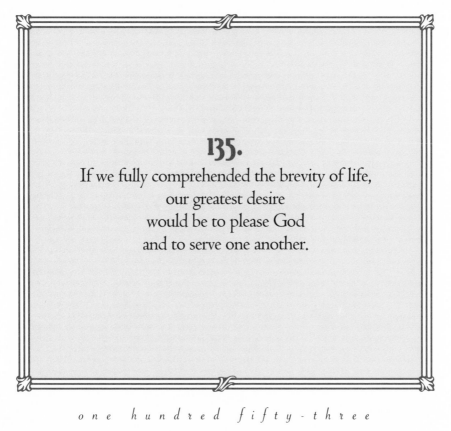

135.

If we fully comprehended the brevity of life,
our greatest desire
would be to please God
and to serve one another.

Love the Lord your God with all your heart and with all your soul and with all your strength.

DEUTERONOMY 6:5

136.

Try not to care so much
about every minute detail that separates you
and your loved ones.
It's all vanity, anyway.
Solomon told us that.

137.
Hold loosely to life
and keep yourself free of willful
and deliberate sin.
That's the key to happiness.

138.
Great beginnings
are not as important
as the way one finishes.

139.

Married life is a marathon, not a sprint.
It is not enough to make a great start
toward long-term marriage.
You will need the determination to keep plugging on,
even when every fiber of your body
longs to quit.

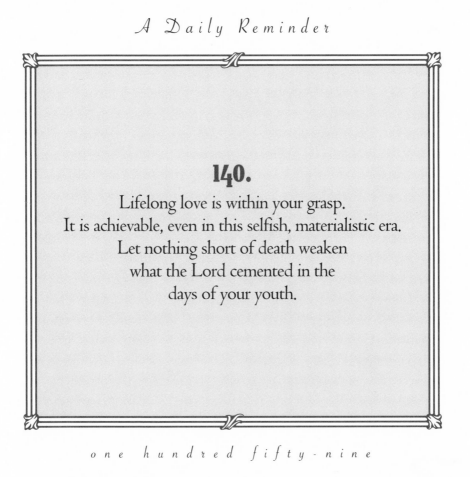

140.

Lifelong love is within your grasp.
It is achievable, even in this selfish, materialistic era.
Let nothing short of death weaken
what the Lord cemented in the
days of your youth.

Above all, love each other deeply,
because love covers a multitude of sins.

1 PETER 4:8